GW00993151

Your journey always
starts with the first step

The Beginning

Facing your own mortality has a life-changing effect on your mental, physical and spiritual beliefs, in your self care, and life choices. At least it did for me.

I am a 73 year old lady with a desire to share my story in the hope it will help anyone on their own journey.

I stopped smoking in 2016, and on the 19th June 2019 I was diagnosed with lung cancer. Although by then I was sure it was not going to be good news. My cough had been troublesome for some time with choking fits, at times causing stress incontinence. Yes I was a Tena lady. It felt as though my body was trying to eject something from my chest. After ignoring the cough for three years I decided I needed a chest x-ray. I dropped into the surgery for an appointment and was seen straight away by the practise nurse. After taking a medical history she gave me an x-ray form. After the x-ray on a Sunday, I was phoned by the respiratory nurse from the hospital to say I had a scan booked for the next Thursday, and an appointment with the chest consultant. With such a quick referral I new it wasn't good news. I was referred to the MDT (multidisciplinary team) meeting. Things then happened quickly and I was on the treadmill of appointments and investigations.

I had two bronchoscopies, the first one didn't give a satisfactory sample. Not a pleasant procedure, but with analgesic spray and a mild sedative it was tolerable. Fitness tests were done on the exercise bike, and breathing apparatus to measure my breathing and lung capacity, and suitability for anaesthetic. I had a mediastinoscopy with biopsy. That involved inserting a camera behind the sternum(breast bone) to sample the lymph nodes. I didn't realise how many lymph nodes lived there until I googled the procedure and saw pictures.

The result was no lymph involvement or metastasis.

I know that all cancers are not the same, and I feel very grateful that mine was resolved so easily with surgery. The tumour was successfully removed in tact with two lobes of my right lung. I was offered chemotherapy and had one cycle of treatment. I then refused any more due to the adverse reactions.

Feeling so ill, with drugs that should be helping me, didn't feel right. I listened to my body meditating on the feelings. I weighed up the odds as I saw them, and decided the conventional way of treatment was not the path I should be on.

I WAS TAKING BACK CONTROL. Something I hadn't felt since the initial diagnosis. I wasn't going to be defined by this illness. Still me, and able to make my own choices on treatment, whatever the outcome might be. My first step was refusing anymore chemotherapy. Scary.

Nobody wants to die, but I felt as though I was with the effects of the chemotherapy drugs. I believe we have the right to choose when given the opportunity. The odds given to me by my consultant oncologist were a 5% chance that the cancer would not return after having chemotherapy. Being told I would have four treatments, to me that meant a 1.25% chance for each cycle of treatment (not very good odds).

My consultant thoracic surgeon told me I was in remission, as the tumour had been removed with no lymph node involvement. This news of course played a part in my decision. I didn't really want chemotherapy in the first place. Knowing that it kills everything in its path as well as any free-floating cancer cells didn't fill me with a feeling of faith in the outcome of treatment. It was an inner feeling of it 'not being right for me'. My body was telling me 'this is not right for you'. So my journey was clear - to be self-healing with nature, and this became my mantra.

Qigong

Qi (or chi) means energy, gong means the skill of. So Qigong is the skill of energy, and the energy we use here is the breath, movement and thought.

It is an ancient Chinese art for health and wellbeing. Grand Masters only taught selective students, usually in the family. Sometimes in secret and this could explain why Qigong has developed independently into so many different schools. Some schools are based on philosophical principles for cultivating internal chi for martial arts, others for healing or spiritual awareness.

Mencius, a great philosopher of 2000 years ago during the Zhou Dynasty of China, stated that "the will is the commander of Chi. Chi is the totality of the body".

This philosopher's insight may be explained as meaning that internal energy can be controlled by the mind. It can be directed to areas or organs of the body by the power of thought. All the cells and tissues of the body, the physiological and mental processes, are the products of energy - chi.

I have practised and taught Qigong for about 30 years. It was vital for my recovery. The breathing has helped with expanding my lungs, especially the only lobe on my right side. The breathing does become a habit, and helps with calming the mind, relieving anxiety and much more. The soft gentle movements are suitable for anyone as you work within your own abilities. As with any task, the more you practise the better you become, and the better the benefits.

According to Chinese medicine, the breathing and movement together move the energy around the body along meridian lines. So any blocked energy in these areas can be gently moved along.

Similar to acupuncture, but you are doing it for yourself with the breath. Numerous benefits include pain control, stress relief, reduction in anxiety and finding that inner feeling of peace.

Sit a while and just breathe.

With the tongue resting in the roof of your mouth, slowly breathe in feeling the lower lungs fill with air as you expand your abdominal muscles.

Slowly breathe out and relax your shoulders and feel your feet sinking into the floor.

Concentrate on your breathing and release all those negative thoughts.

Empty your mind. Let it become fluid.

As you slowly breathe in, follow the breath right down into the tummy and slowly breathe out through the mouth fully before you inhale again.

This can be practised anywhere at any time, either standing up or sitting down, even lying down. Some people find this breathing can help with getting to sleep. Practised daily it soon becomes a habit and can be used to calm the mind or thoughts in stressful situations.

Shinrin-Yoku Forest Bathing

Shinrin-Yoku is a Japanese concept of health. This literally fell into my lap while I was recuperating from my surgery. I wasn't looking for it, and in fact I'd never heard of it. Sometimes, I believe things that are meant for us appear at the right time, and it made complete sense to me that nature was vital for my own healing.

I think in general, people feel the benefits of spending time in nature. A long walk either in the forest, by the sea, along the canal path can lift your mood, release tension and relax the mind.

The World Health Organisation describes stress as the 21st century health epidemic. After preliminary studies on the benefits of shin-rin yoku, it was in 2004 that scientific research was started in Japan by Dr.Qing Li. His book "Shin-rin Yoku the

Art and Science of Forest Bathing" gives a comprehensive understandable account of his research and the development of forest bathing.

So get out there to a forest near you. Remember, this is not a hike. You need to be IN the forest. (This now suits me as I need to be a lot slower than I was).

Open your senses, see the different colours of the forest, feel the colour of the forest as it wraps around you.

Dr. Qing Li states in his aforementioned book that "one of the most important elements of shin-rin yoku is the fragrance the trees release, their phytoncides. When you walk in the forest you are breathing in its healing power".

The phytoncides are antibacterial, and released by trees to protect themselves from harmful germs and insects. Up-to-date research now shows how phytoncides can help us by reducing cortisol, one of the stress hormones, and can effectively work on the white blood cells (NK cells which are anti cancer protiens), so boosting the immune system and helping to reduce immune related illnesses. We inhale phytoncides from the forest so the breathing is important to focus on.

We have a symbiotic relationship with trees. We breathe in oxygen and breathe out carbon dioxide. Trees breathe in carbon dioxide and breathe out oxygen. We are supportive of each other, healing with nature. There is something about being in the forest that lifts your spirit. Connecting with nature feels right. As we are all made of energy we can find peace, strength and calmness to deal with the stresses of life.

"There is a sense in the tree which feels your love and responds to it. It does not respond or show its pleasure in our way or in any way we can now understand".

Prentice Mulford 1834-1891 author of "Thoughts are Things"

Touch the trees

Hug a tree

Feel the bark

Take your shoes off and feel the earth of the forest.

Geosmin, the earthy musty smell of the soil, is released when we kick the leaves in autumn.

Taste the forest, drink from the stream, eat the nuts and berries (but make sure you know what's safe).

Listen to the forest, hear the birds and animals, hear the wind as it gently moves the branches and blows the leaves.

And don't forget your sixth sense. Sensing the energy, as you slowly breathe in and slowly breathe out while sitting under a tree.

You can connect with the essence that can be difficult to describe, but you know it is there, something much bigger than ourselves.

Wandering through the forest
Sharing the energy
Controlling the breath
Slowly breathing in
Slowly breathing out
Feel the shoulders relax
All the tension drains away
Hearing the silence
As you travel deeper into the forest
Wrapped in the beautiful colours of nature
The wind stirs the branches and leaves
Bringing scents to sooth the mind
And lift the soul
Connecting with the essence of life.

Seek out a tree
And let it teach you stillness

Eckhart Tolle
Author and spiritual teacher

Look deeper into nature and
then you will understand
everything better.

Albert Einstein

Diet

I am not a forager, and do not suggest these fungi are edible, but mushrooms are full of vitamin D and are one of my favourite breakfasts. They are also beneficial in boosting the immune system.

My immune system may have been compromised with only one round of chemotherapy, so I follow a balanced healthy diet and eat fresh fruit and vegetables every day. Green tea is my drink of choice. It's an antioxidant, which reduces the risk of many cancers, including lung cancer. It contains phytonutrients which boost the hormones that make you feel good, which is another reason to drink it. Researching food values and the best type of food for me on this healing journey, it was good to remind myself of all the vitamins and minerals that are readily available in affordable everyday fruit and vegetables. It's all down to choices and cutting out the sugary processed junk food. Cancers feed on sugar so I don't add sugar to anything now.

"What you find at the end of your fork is more powerful than anything you'll find at the bottom of a pill bottle"

Dr. Mark Hyman
American physician and author
Director of the Ultra Wellness Centre

Finding fungi on
walks through the forest

Salmon with roast veg

Positive Mind

Given the right environment the body can heal itself.

    Nature's natural medicine
    Sunshine
    Water
    Exercise
    Laughter
    Good friends and family
    Rest and sleep

Lifestyle choices are an important element in building up the body's defences. These all work in harmony in balancing the immune system. The energy systems of the meridians, chakras and the body's aura can give an indication of imbalance to those working with energy.

No single therapy or food can resolve your health problems. It's about using what works best for you. Working on yourself, to resolve your state of mind, having a positive outlook and choosing tools that work for you.

I have a good friend who came every afternoon while I was recouperating from surgery. We walked down the street to keep me mobile. This meant I had to get dressed to go out. She pushed me a little bit more each day, "lets walk to the next gate". It was good psychology and got me moving a lot sooner than I would have if left to my own devises.

Having an arsenal of therapies to balance your mind and body doesn't have to be expensive.

There is lots of information on YouTube and the internet for your mental and physical health and wellbeing, and a lot of it is free.

Don't be afraid to take an unfamiliar path. They can sometimes take you to the best places.

If you are unable to get out into the forest or countryside, it can be beneficial to bring the outside in.

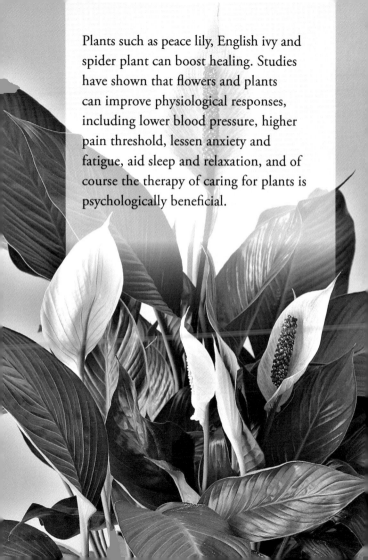

Plants such as peace lily, English ivy and spider plant can boost healing. Studies have shown that flowers and plants can improve physiological responses, including lower blood pressure, higher pain threshold, lessen anxiety and fatigue, aid sleep and relaxation, and of course the therapy of caring for plants is psychologically beneficial.

Drip essential oils onto pine cones to bring the scent of the forest into your room.

Every day may not be good
But there's something good
in every day.

It's ok to have a
'nothing to do' day
It's ok to have a day
doing nothing.

Reflexology

I have trained in reflexology but no longer practice it. Being aware of the benefits my clients received over the years, this is one of the complimentary therapies I have turned to in my own healing programme.

Treatments were interrupted in the lock-down of 2020-2021, and I could feel the difference for not having had my treatments. Like Qigong and shinrin-yoku it is an energy therapy. The therapist stimulates the nerve endings in the feet which are related to systems of the body. It can be both relaxing and stimulating at the same time. A good therapist is able to detect areas that are out of balance so you are able to adjust your healing programme to suit your needs.

It has certainly helped with my back problem. Wear and tear from nursing has left me with bulging discs in my lumber four and five vertebra, with some intermittent sciatic pain to my left leg. This always feels better after a reflexology treatment. I still have some neuralgia to my right chest, I believe from nerve damage with the surgery to remove my lung. This has eased over the past few years and is no longer a problem, now more of an irritation.

The therapy of touch in whatever form - massage, reiki, reflexology, a hug - has huge benefits to mental wellbeing and the feeling of being cared for. Self-care is an important part of my life now.

I am important.
You are important.

Affirmations

Using a short sentence or phrase daily reaffirms the positive state of mind. It can change the way you think and make positive changes in your life. It can be anything you think you need in your life.

I am healthy
I am well
I am positive
I can do it
I am the best I can be in everything I do
I will succeed
I am beautiful

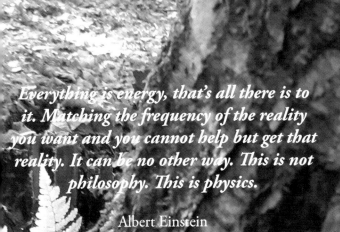

Everything is energy, that's all there is to it. Matching the frequency of the reality you want and you cannot help but get that reality. It can be no other way. This is not philosophy. This is physics.

Albert Einstein

Meditation

This doesn't have to be difficult. You don't have to sit cross-legged on the floor. A comfortable chair with your feet on the floor is suitable. The aim is to quieten the mind. I have practised meditation for a number of years. Sometimes using the breath to focus on, sometimes using guided meditation, or just listening to quiet mood music. With the guided meditation it is important to choose a voice you can listen comfortably to. The right accent and intonation of the voice all adds to the experience and enjoyment. It can help with reducing anxiety, lowering blood pressure, improving concentration and with sleep problems. If you find your mind wandering onto other thoughts then don't reprimand yourself, bring your focus back to the breathing.

You are aiming to achieve a liquid mind. Let go of any thoughts, become more fluid. If you have not meditated before start with a short three to five minutes. Building up the length of your practise will help you to find the right balance of time for your meditation.

Another way to start is to light a candle and place it in front of you. Look at the flame and then close your eyes. Hold the image of the candle in your minds eye. All your thoughts are concentrated on this flame.

There is a visual meditation in the chapter on shinrin-yoku. Keep reading it until you are familiar with the words or record it so you can listen to it any time, any where. Stop pedalling like mad. Practise meditation to become calmer and find some peace.

Exercise

I feel this is important to mention, as it can often be overlooked. I look at it like this: We breathe in and oxygen is taken into the lungs. It is absorbed into the blood and pumped round the body by the heart, feeding all the cells and tissues with oxygen. Isn't the body wonderful doing all this without us having to think about it? The lymphatic system has no pump, so we have to exercise to 'pump' the lymph around the body. So, by moving the arms and legs, we are using our muscles to squeeze the lymph glands and channels to move the lymph around the body. This is important to help drain and balance the body fluids. As part of the immune system it also helps fight infections. Your lymphatic system removes waste like viruses, bacteria and abnormal cells that can lead to cancer. So by exercising you can help it do its job.

I have two dogs and walk them daily. Usually an hour's walk. We love trips to the forest. Clumber Park is not far away and I aim for trips out at least every month or more frequently. It's a great place for shinrin-yoku. I can sit when I need to rest, and just breathe in the benefit of the trees. I have this year discovered aqua fit, and this suits me, as being in the water supports my body and I don't get short of breath. I can certainly feel the benefits and feel more toned. I am still teaching two Qigong classes a week and practising daily for myself.

So try some form of exercise. Work within your abilities, even if it's chair exercise. Lift your arms and legs gently. Walk around the room or walk to your gate if that is all you can manage. There's no judgement here, you can build on your successes each day.

Reflections

We all need time to reflect on life. As long as we don't stay there, and make sure we come back to the now.

I used music in my convalescence. I must have played every CD I had, right back to Jim Reeves. What? At that time I wasn't fit for much else. Concentration was nil. It was at this time that I was cured of my soap opera addiction. As an avid fan of all the soaps I could no longer be bothered about dramas and the imaginary lives of others.

Listening to the music was very cathartic. I was releasing past memories, both good and bad, which helped to build up my strength and determination to become something of my former self. I shed a lot of tears for all the wrong reasons (and a few right ones).

I had a lot of support from friends and family. My sister did meals on wheels for me until I was able to cook for myself again. My niece and a friend walked the dogs for me until I had built up the strength to do it myself. My niece also drove me to Sheffield numerous times for appointments and whizzed me round Tesco in a wheelchair. Not forgetting my friend I mentioned earlier who walked with me every afternoon. My thanks also to Amy for reading my first draft of this book.

The constipation was resolved when I cut down on the painkillers and started walking further. And the weight loss, down to 7stone 4 pounds, was soon built back up once my appetite was back to normal. This of course all took time, but by Christmas of 2019 I was walking the dogs and cooking for myself.

A very sad part of these reflections is that I lost a dear friend to lung cancer in November of 2020. We went to school

together, and we did our nurse training together. I was a bridesmaid when she got married. She was the first person I told about my diagnosis, and about three to four weeks later she was diagnosed with the same thing. We thought we were facing and fighting this together, but it wasn't to be and in the late summer of that year there was a marked deterioration in her health, with secondaries to the other lung and her brain. After being in hospital for two weeks she came home to die, her husband and son with her.

As you can imagine my emotions were all over the place at this time. Feelings of gratitude for my own health, and also fear for my own health. Feelings of loss for a good friend and the usual "why? why?" when we don't understand the way of the world.

I have worked through these feelings, initially with Empowered in Nature CIC. They are a company of therapists delivering workshops for bereavement and loss, anxiety, emotional eating. They run forest schools for grown ups. Workshops are usually delivered outside in nature. It was this that appealed to me when I came across it. Again this was something that just appeared when I needed it.

Being in nature is certainly a must for me. I find it therapeutic, calming and empowering in a strange kind of way. I have worked through my feelings of loss and bereavement with Empowered in Nature CIC, using a natural setting with a very supportive group.

Facing death and being able to talk about it has helped me to manage my own emotions around this subject. Having arrangements in place now has liberated me. Giving myself permission to live my life in the now.

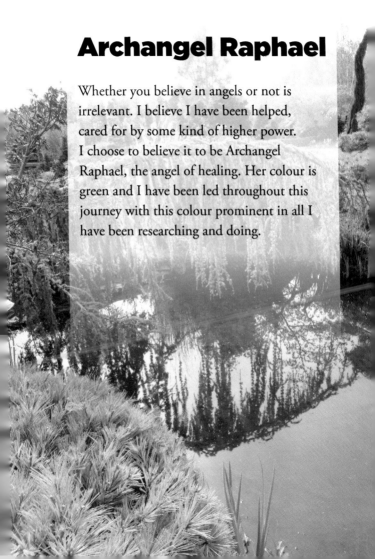

Archangel Raphael

Whether you believe in angels or not is
irrelevant. I believe I have been helped,
cared for by some kind of higher power.
I choose to believe it to be Archangel
Raphael, the angel of healing. Her colour is
green and I have been led throughout this
journey with this colour prominent in all I
have been researching and doing.

Directory

The following are books and services that have helped me. They may lead the way for you to find what is right for you on your healing journey.

Books

Chi-Gung Harnessing the Power of the Universe *Daniel Reed*

Change Your Thoughts - Change Your Life *Dr Wayne Dyer*

A New Earth - Create a Better Life *Eckhart Tolle*

The Secret, The Power *Rhonda Byrne*

Shinrin-Yoku the Art and Science of Forest Bathing *Dr. Qing LI*

Forest Bathing *Sarah Ivens*

Your Guide to Forest Bathing *M. Amos Clifford*

Cygnus Books. A library of mind body spirit literature, music and videos. *Found on the internet.*

Therapies

Qigong

My classes are Mondays 6pm to 7pm at the Pavilion Belton. Thursday 10.30am to 11.30am at the Ivanhoe Centre Conisborough. Tel: 07540 478401

Reflexology

Holistic Harmony. Jayne also has other therapies available.
www.holisticharmony.info.

Shinrin-yoku

There are guides trained in this who lead walks, but I just go myself and absorb the energy. Sit when I want to and meditate.

Meditation / Mindfulness

Wild Orange. Carole has a wide range of courses to offer. One which may suit you.
www.wild-orange.co.uk

This book is a guide for you to start research on your own healing journey, whatever your health problem may be. There are answers out there if you take control of your own healing.

The End

It's not really the end until the lid is nailed down on the coffin. I am still in remission three years after my diagnosis, and I hope to have a few more years to experience life in this mad world. I have still not seen a G.P. - but that's another story.

I came across this poem when I was researching something else. I thought it very relevant and should be included in my book. Written by a peasant from a small village in Mexico, a lady with foresight into healing using natural elements.